TOTALLY ABSURD
INVENTIONS

cranium cooler

FIG. 1

TOTALLY ABSURD INVENTIONS

all-terrain stroller

America's Goofiest Patents

5.125 in

25 in

ed VanCleave

Andrews McMeel
Publishing

Kansas City

Totally Absurd Inventions: America's Goofiest Patents

For information, write Andrews McMeel Publishing,
an Andrews McMeel Universal company, 4520 Main Street,
Kansas City, Missouri 64111.

01 02 03 04 05 BIN 10 9 8 7 6 5 4 3 2 1

Library of Congress Cataloging-in-Publication Data

Vancleave, Ted.
Totally absurd inventions: America's goofiest patents / Ted Vancleave.
     p. cm.
ISBN 0-7407-1025-7 (pbk.)
     1. Inventions—United States. 2. Inventions—United States— Humor.
     3. Patents—United States. 4. Patents—United States— Humor. I. Title.
T212.V36 2001
609.73—dc21   00-049572

Book design by Holly Camerlinck

——— **Attention: Schools and Businesses** ———

Andrews McMeel books are available at quantity discounts with
bulk purchase for educational, business, or sales promotional use.
For information, please write to: Special Sales Department,
Andrews McMeel Publishing, 4520 Main Street, Kansas City, Missouri 64111.

To my mother and father for their immense love and support.

To Charleen for her laughter and nudge.

And to the inventors of the world, who think outside the box,
often way outside the box. It would be a boring place without you.

Contents

I love the creative process and admire each and every inventor featured in this book. I admire them for their courage and tenacity to steadfastly stand by their ideas and actually patent them. After all, the United States patent process is a long and tricky one, filled with exacting rules, attorneys, revisions, and rejections. U.S. patents can often take over two years to process and cost more than $2,500. An inventor will spend his time and money pursuing a patent with absolutely no guarantee of success. And if one is indeed awarded a patent, he shouldn't expect the world to beat a path to his door. Only about 3 percent of all U.S. patents become commercially available, viable products. The rest reside in the vast U.S. Patent Repository, collecting dust but serving as a permanent record of genius as recognized by the United States government.

Finding these gems is no easy task. The Patent Office issues over 150,000 patents each year and less than 150 of them are wacky enough to be Totally Absurd

Inventions. The process of discovering these goofy inventions is tedious and requires flipping through book after book, reviewing thousands of boring and actually useful patents. The payoff is stumbling across a gem such as "Cow Gas" whose official patent title is "System for Measuring Metabolic Gas Emissions from Animals" or "Super Trash Man," officially titled "Flexible Receptacle for Collecting and Transporting Loose Debris."

Please join me now for a glimpse into the mind of genius. Indulge yourself and enjoy the most incredible and humorous patents in America. Who knows, you, too, may be inspired to dream big and get your own wacky patent.

cranium cooler

FIG. 1

TOTALLY

Chapter 1

ABSURD

all-terrain stroller

INVENTIONS

America's Goofiest Patents

25 *in*

GOOFY!

diaper alarm

Diaper Alarm

US Patent No. 4,205,672
Issue Date 1980

Are you tired of sticking your fingers down a wet diaper for moisture verification? How else can you know if your baby's diaper is wet again? If you had the Diaper Alarm, you could become a quick-change artist and keep your fingers dry! Simply clamp the sensor onto the diaper, and when your baby wets, mild electrical conduction along your baby's skin activates blinking lights and an alarm. Is it just us, or do you think there is something a little wrong with combining babies, electricity, and water?

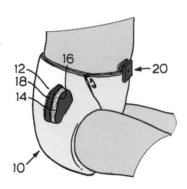

Fowl Spoon

US Patent No. 4,779,344
Issue Date 1988

Has feeding time for your little tot become a burden because she refuses to open her mouth? What should you do when prying her food trap open is only a fantasy and not a real option? It's time to bring in the big guns! It's time for "Rubber Lips, the Spoon Puppet"! To use, stick your finger (#38) into what the inventor calls the "rear finger receiving channel" of Rubber Lips. Then make a few quacking noises, shake your finger to and fro, and behold a child with gaping mouth. Not that she suddenly became hungry, she's in awe of your mastery of puppetry. So be fast and shove that spoon in before the awe wears thin, and repeat the procedure twenty-five times.

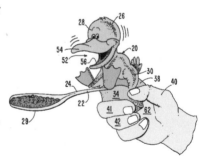

Bubble Head

US Patent No. 4,663,785
Issue Date 1987

In the sport of boxing, boxers, especially bad boxers, take a lot of blows to the head. Too many whacks to the noggin can rattle their brains. What boxers need is better head protection. Enter the Bubble Head, a clear plastic bag filled with shock-absorbing translucent fluid. But wait: There's more! Each Bubble Head comes complete with a pressure-sensitive reservoir filled with red dye. Every time an opponent scores a blow to the head, red dye is released into the fluid-filled helmet. At the end of the fight, the boxers retain their brains and the reddest head loses.

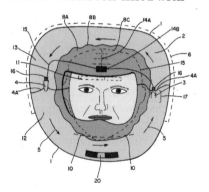

Foot Elevator

US Patent No. 4,586,207
Issue Date 1986

We've all seen it on summer vacation, and it's not pretty. Shins burned to a fine lobster red, calves white as a fish belly. Two-toned legs have never been the fashion, but short of climbing onto a rotisserie, how can you easily get an even leg tan? We thought you'd never ask! Enter the Foot Elevator, designed to raise your legs off the sand so you can achieve an oh-so-desirable, all-over tan without turning. To use, take the plastic tootsie lift and stick it in the sand. Next, line up your real toes with the plastic toes and ease your feet into the heel rest. Now, if we could just find a Neck Elevator and a Butt Elevator . . .

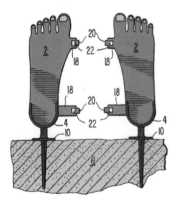

Alarm Fork

US Patent No. 5,421,089
Issue Date 1995

Who doesn't like to eat? Whether it's a big juicy steak or tofu casserole, everyone likes to chow down. But Americans can be a gluttonous lot, and obesity abounds around our towns. Why? Because you people are eating too fast! Quit inhaling your food! Slow down, take a break, and give your food some time to settle. Slower eating leads to feeling full before you've devoured an entire ten-course meal. Less food, less weight gain. And we're here to help, with the amazing Alarm Fork. The rules: You can eat only when your fork gives you the green light. That's right, once you've shoveled some food into your mouth, the sensors cue the fork to emit a red light. And you know what that means: *Stop!* Now wait, tick, tick, tick, tick . . . ding! Green light, take a bite.

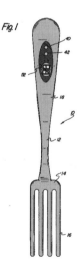

Fig. 1

Sleep Sponge

US Patent No. 5,199,124
Issue Date 1993

Some people should not sleep on their stomachs. Why not snooze on your tummy? you might ask. Well, we're not exactly sure, but the inventor must have had a good reason. The Sleep Sponge is a wedge-shaped foam cushion attached to a superhero-style belt. When you're ready to hit the sack, strap on your belly belt and bid the day adieu. You may want to wear it watching TV because it makes an excellent bedtime-snack tray. As an added bonus, sleepwalkers now have a built-in crash bumper. But be careful—your cat will find the Sleep Sponge simply irresistible!

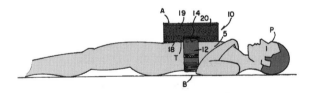

Tongue Zapper

US Patent No. 6,017,262
Issue Date 2000

Frogs and lizards (and members of certain rock bands) have the unique ability to extend a very long tongue and zap their prey at astonishing speeds. Kids are fascinated by them. What young boy hasn't walked around with his tongue sticking out, imitating a lizard? (Okay, so maybe I *was* a weird child.) The Tongue Zapper can fulfill a child's dream of catching bugs with his tongue and possibly save thousands of dollars in therapy costs when he grows to become a more well adjusted adult. Just don't be surprised when little Johnny sits down at the dinner table and starts using the dish of peas as target practice. Hey, if he gets real good at it, you can toss the fly swatter!

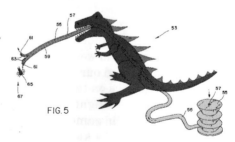

FIG. 5

Fingernail Fanatic

US Patent No. 6,016,812
Issue Date 2000

According to the inventor, "In this modern world, we are constantly being judged by our appearance. Whether it is our personality, intelligence, wit, or good demeanor we want to emphasize and be judged by, personal hygiene seems to play an even bigger role than ever before, notwithstanding our other traits. Today, hard work and industry are not enough for a man to impress others. Gone are the days of old when a man could come home to his wife after a hard day's work, smelling of foul odors and being covered from head to toe in dirt, with no negative repercussion. Instead, we live in a highly sanitized and glamorized society in which images of finely dressed and well-coiffed models are continuously being thrust into our view as well as our collective psyche." He goes on to say, "For thousands of years, people have been fighting dirty fingernails much like they hunted wild game in cave-man days—manually, with the blade of a knife. While this may work in some cases, such as where the dirt is easily dislodged, it

Goofy!

presupposes a certain level of coordination while handling a knife. Once again, today's modern man is both better educated and less adept with a knife." Okay, let's get serious here, folks; our inventor has spent way too much time thinking about clean fingernails, their history, and their impact on society at large. But such a detailed mind has brought us a foolproof, completely automated machine for cleaning that hard substance growing from the ends of our digits. The Fingernail Fanatic has an amazing array of features, including, but not limited to (a little attorneyspeak there), motor driven, finely tuned oscillating brushes, fine jets of aqueous solution, and finger-alignment tunnels to maintain proper digit orientation in the plane of the scrubbing zone. Wow, we're impressed, but the inventor should think about getting out of the lab a little more often.

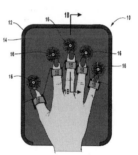

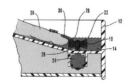

Floating Furniture

US Patent No. 4,888,836
Issue Date 1989

Tired of looking at your table and chairs all day long? Does your bed take up entirely too much space? This invention will allow you to roam your home with no obstacles during the day and sleep easily at night! This lighter-than-air furniture can be levitated with helium gas and stored on your ceiling when you're not using it! Need a nap? Just grab the tether rope (#34) and pull your bed down from the ceiling. Imagine, you will never have to make your bed or clear off the dinner table again!

Simply inflate your furnishings, and messy beds and untidy tables are out of sight! Just be sure the pets don't get trapped between the sofa and the ceiling.

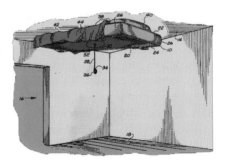

Spitting Duck

US Patent No. 6,006,372
Issue Date 1999

Someday we're going to run out of trees to make toilet paper, and then we'll be in deep cacadoodoo. Fortunately, there's an inventor who already has a solution. A solution of soap and perfume, that is. The Spitting Duck is designed to fit most toilets, and instead of using toilet paper, you lift the duck's bill and a strategically placed nozzle will spray your buttooski with the secret cleaning formula. Details are sketchy, but the dazed look on our ducky friend's face probably comes from sitting on the toilet all day.

Flood Bag

US Patent No. 4,315,535
Issue Date 1982

When El Niño was causing floods around the world, we thought this invention would be appropriate. We've all seen the television footage of cars up to their headlights in muddy floodwaters. Vehicles are often abandoned because waters rise quickly and become too deep to drive through safely. What we don't see is the ravage a flood

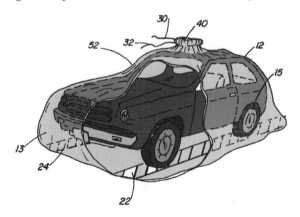

causes to a car once the waters recede. The engine and interior are full of gritty, gooey mud that clings to everything. Usually the motor is ruined and the vehicle is declared a complete loss. This giant plastic bag is the ultimate in vehicle flood protection, and it's so simple to use. The interior of the bag has markings to guide you as you drive your car into it. Exit the vehicle and pull the sides of the bag up over your car. Next, pull the drawstring tightly, closing the opening. The key here is to make sure you leave a space large enough to allow air to escape as the floodwaters ensue. Otherwise trapped air will fill the bag, and your car will float off into the sunset.

Greenhouse Helmet

US Patent No. 4,605,000
Issue Date 1986

Welcome to the Greenhouse Helmet, your own personal biosphere! This invention consists of a sealed plastic dome, plants on tiny shelves, and speakers and a microphone for communication with the outside world. The mini greenhouse is designed to allow the user to breathe the oxygen given off by plants growing near his ears. The inventor never really says why you may need the measly amount of oxygen given off by a couple of cacti. Maybe this invention will provide the extra edge needed by future Olympic athletes to win the Gold.

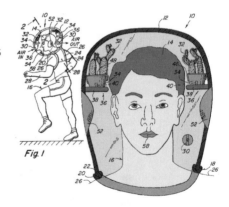

Fig. I

Head Boom

US Patent No. 4,249,712
Issue Date 1979

Let's say you have a job that requires you to look down all day. You could be a jeweler, a draftsperson (do they still exist?), or someone that has to study fine detail. These types of jobs can strain your neck and your back, making work very uncomfortable. But never fear, the Head Boom is here! This wonderful work-aid clamps onto your desk with the adjustable boom extending to your face. You simply rest your forehead on the boom's soft sponge (#21) and work your little heart out in comfort. And *no sleeping!*

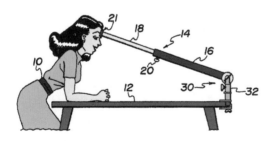

Redundant Recumbent

US Patent No. 6,021,535

Issue Date 2000

Sitting at a computer all day can be a pain in the neck . . . and the back and the wrists. The human anatomy just wasn't designed to sit in a chair all day whacking away at a keyboard. We need support and support is what you get with the Redundant Recumbent computer workstation. This thing fully adjusts to every type of body known to the human race, and it looks sooo comfy. It's a great idea, but try to get your bumbling

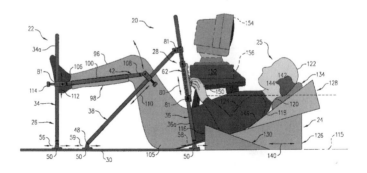

boss to sign off on this one! We can hear it now: "If *you* have one, then we have to buy them for everyone." Can you imagine walking into an office and finding everyone lying down on the job? Hey, look at the money the company will save, since everyone will need only a three-foot-high cubicle! And again—no sleeping!

Meditation Bag

US Patent No. 4,330,889
Issue Date 1982

If you meditate or sleep (and who doesn't?), we recommend the marvelous "Meditation and Sleeping Bag." It's warm and cozy for snowy peaks and chilly caves yet large enough to accommodate useful yoga props. Designed for sitting or reclining, the Meditation Bag includes a drawstring enclosure exposing only your face to fresh air and reality. If sitting in a cold room watching *Matlock* reruns helps you reach your own state of nirvana, hey, we're not passing judgement. To reach the deepest state of bliss, close your eyes, say good night, and roll over.

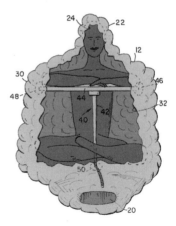

Hi ho, hi ho, it's off to hike we go. Outdoor exercise and activities can be good for your health, but you have to use some protection. No, not that kind of protection. Prolonged exposure to intense heat and sunlight can cause sunburn, sunstroke, dehydration, and skin cancer (the sofa is looking good right now). But never fear, Floating Shade is here! This helium-filled, balloonlike sunscreen hovers over you, creating your own personal hands-free solar eclipse. Got a crowd at the family picnic? Get the jumbo model; it'll cast a shadow bigger than a UFO Mothership!

Ski Tutor

US Patent No. 4,545,575
Issue Date 1985

So, you want to learn to ski? Are your friends migrating to Aspen, while you're left in the lurch due to a complete lack of skiing ability? Tradition dictates that the best way to learn to ski is to get out on the slopes and practice. Hey, forget about fresh air, beautiful views, and fresh powdered snow; the Ski Tutor will teach you how to ski in the most absurd way possible! Strap yourself into the harness which is attached to a movable frame. This will provide balance when you inevitably stumble and fall. Next, slide your feet into the imitation skis and glide your feet forward and backward. The fun just never stops. Now you know the training secret of Olympic skiers (shhhh!).

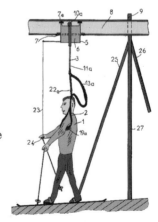

Ultimate Lounger

US Patent No. 3,969,776
Issue Date 1976

Is the sizzling summer heat causing you to have a personal meltdown? Do you feel that if it gets any hotter, you may just spontaneously combust? You don't have a pool, and you're tired of filling the bathtub with ice cubes so you can cool down. What to do? What to do? Well, it's time to run to your favorite superstore and buy yourself the Ultimate Lounger! Ahhhh, picture this: It's a hot, steamy afternoon and you're livin' large in your poor-man's pool. Cool drink and favorite book by your side, reclining backrest, adjustable umbrella, stunning side-panel graphics, and your cherished rubber ducky. And the best news yet—you look so doggone groovy. Just remember the pool owners' creed: If you don't pee in our pool, we won't swim in your toilet. Words to live by.

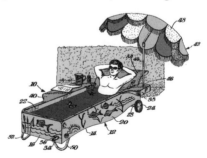

Thumb-Sucking Inhibitor

US Patent No. **4,665,907**
Issue Date **1987**

Have you been attempting to break your thumb-sucking habit, but nothing seems to curb your fixation? Have you had just about enough of your friends and coworkers teasing you about your favorite way to relax? Well, Linus, now you can successfully crack your thumb-sucking addiction with the Thumb-Sucking Inhibitor! The "Apparatus for Inhibiting Digit Sucking" is an attractive way to get rid of an unsightly habit. Simply attach the steel girder and metal support beams to the desired appendage. Now suck it, we dare you!

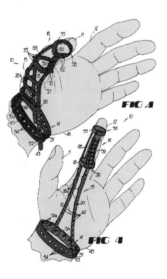

Wiz Pouch	US Patent No. 5,819,331
	Issue Date 1998

Why don't home bathrooms have separate urinals? We suppose it's because of lack of space in what's usually the home's tiniest room. The solution? The Wiz Pouch. This curious invention converts a standard toilet into a multireceptacle device. The Wiz Pouch utilizes a two-piece toilet lid that has a rubberized flexible pouch sandwiched in the middle. When not in use, the urinal is folded flat behind cover #40, hiding it from view and allowing you to use the toilet in a normal fashion. To use the Wiz Pouch, pull down the cover and the urinal will pop open. Our question is this: If guys can't hit the toilet now, as large as it is, what kind of untidiness is this small target going to create? Ladies, let's have a show of hands. . . . The nays have it.

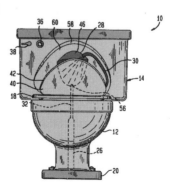

Shoulder Saddle

US Patent No. 3,698,608
Issue Date 1972

Does your tiny tyke like to ride on your shoulders, but you find it hard to hang on to fidgety feet? Have you recently discovered that your neck is starting to get a little diaper rash? Then you need the Shoulder Saddle! The saddle's plastic yoke fits over your head, and the breast plate and back plate evenly distribute the load. The breast plate also makes an effective kick guard. Now, if you can just get your petite passenger to understand that slapping your ears repeatedly doesn't mean "Go faster"!

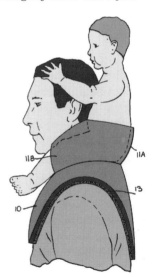

Toilet Landing Lights

US Patent No. 5,263,209
Issue Date 1993

What happens when you go to the bathroom in the middle of the night? Do you turn on the light and squint, trying not to blind yourself, or poke around in complete darkness? Have you ever fallen into the toilet because the seat was up, but, "who knew," it was too dark to see, or heard any complaints about missed targets? Well, not anymore with the extraordinary Toilet Landing Lights! This unprecedented bathroom brainchild can save you from a very embarrassing breakfast conversation by illuminating your way after bedtime, and you know what we mean. Waterproof indirect lighting is placed under the rim of the toilet, adding a beautiful almost mystical glow to the throne. A switch attached to the lid can signal heads-up or safe landing ahead. We suggest pulsing blue airport landing lights to bring you down safely.

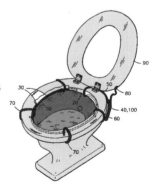

Crunch Protector

US Patent No. 4,986,433
Issue Date 1991

Okay, let's have a show of hands. Who likes soggy cereal? Just as we thought, a couple of troublemakers out there, but most of you don't enjoy limp flakes. It's a view you share with the inventor of the Crunch Protector. The concept is simple: Separate your dry cereal from your wet milk until right before you eat it for true "just in time" delivery. To use, fill the base of the milk bowl with sand (#21) to counter the weight of the cereal in the upper bowl (#23). Now urge an appropriate amount of cereal down the chute (#14) to the awaiting milk in the lower bowl (#22) and eat. Continue to urge and eat while keeping your Rice Krispy and your Cap'ns Crunchy.

cranium cooler

FIG. 1

TOTALLY
ABSURD
INVENTIONS
America's Goofiest Patents

all-terrain stroller

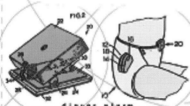
diaper alarm

Chapter 2

IT'S ALIVE!

FIG. 1

Pet Shower

US Patent No. 5,632,231
Issue Date 1995

The inventor pretty well sums up the reason for his pet shower: "The object is to provide . . . a system for cleaning dogs and cats without the hassle of a person chasing the pet, holding the pet, getting wet from the pet, being bitten by the pet, and getting scratched by the pet." We bet that when you let the pet out of the shower, you will get all of the above from the pet. Woof.

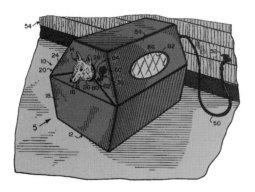

Cricket Gun

US Patent No. | 5,103,585
Issue Date | 1992

Have you ever gone fishing using crickets as bait? Does it bug you when you open the bait bucket and all of the crickets take this opportune moment to flee for their lives? This bait-bucket thing is a two-handed operation, and you know what that means—you may have to set your beer down for a moment, causing you to lose concentration. Well, we have the solution for all of your fishin' and cricket needs, the Cricket Gun! To use, just load the gun with a multitude of frisky crickets and when you are ready to feed the fish, pull the trigger and snatch the little fella as he flies by. He'll be so bewildered by his blast from the past that he may not resist having you get your hook into him. We do suggest one note of caution: Fat crickets make a messy jam.

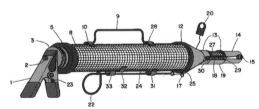

Baby Shower

US Patent No. 5,033,131
Issue Date 1991

It's Alive!

Kids poop. Oh, we know this may come as a surprise to some of you, but —it happens. It can be a difficult task, to say the least, to try to hold on to a squirmy one-year-old and rinse off his tiny behind. The shower head is too high up, the tub is too big, and half-pint wants to run around or plop down. You're trying to corral your writhing tyke with one hand while attempting target practice on a small moving posterior with the other. Whew, we're worn out just thinking about it. But never fear, Baby Shower is here! The BS snaps onto the side of your bathtub and is fully adjustable for poopers of all sizes. Place you know who, you know where, and the gentle warm-water spray will make cleanup time a joy. Okay, maybe *joy* is a little strong, but, hey, don't blame us, we're toilet trained.

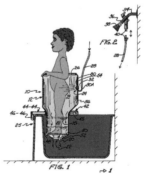

Goose Head

US Patent No. 5,197,216
Issue Date 1991

Yo Goose Head, why you trying to kill the birds? Well, the birds don't want to meet with fowl play, so they keenly avoid hunters. Hunters must fool the birds into thinking that there's nothing unusual about a big weird guy wearing a superhero cape and a plastic goose head molded into his baseball cap. In order to fool the birds, the inventor suggests the hunter move his head from side to side and flap his cape a little to simulate a happy goose. We think anyone wearing this getup should be banned not only from owning guns, but also from breeding. We're rootin' for the goose.

Bat Boy

US Patent No. 5,713,603
Issue Date 1998

Look, up in the sky! It's a bird! It's a plane! No, it's In-Line Bat Boy! Able to leap tall speed bumps in a single bound, our superhero and his helmetlike hair scare the horse hockey out of common criminals. But all kidding aside, this is the goofiest-looking outfit we've seen in ages. Our happy hero has mastered the wind and simply needs to flap his mechanical wings to make in-line skating a breeze.

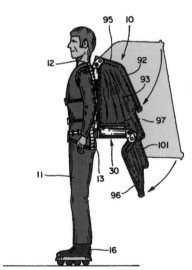

Water Bed Womb

US Patent No. 4,662,010
Issue Date 1987

How do you relieve tension? Do you jump into the Jacuzzi or take a long, hot bath? These can be very relaxing routines. The only problem is that pretty soon you start to wrinkle. Looking like a prune is not very cool. Plus, sleeping in a hot tub is not recommended by the American Lifeguard Association! What should you do to relax? Introducing the ultimate in relaxation for all of you stress-afflicted people out there. Now you can relieve tension and stress while you sleep, wrinkle free! The

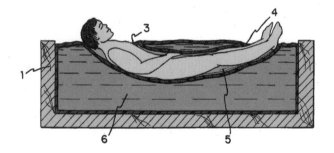

Water Bed Womb is a waterproof vinyl body bag sealed inside a water bed. Go ahead; slide into the Water Bed Womb, and at once you are suspended in and surrounded by warm, soothing water. The best news yet: You can stay inside as long as you want because you remain completely dry!

It's Alive!

Fish Bath

US Patent No. 4,364,132
Issue Date 1982

What happens when you combine an aquarium and a bathtub? You bathe in a fish-lover's paradise encircled by live seafood swimming round and round inside your transparent tub. According to the inventor, "The bather will be literally surrounded by aquarium creatures . . . while taking his or her bath. At other times, the size of the aquarium provides a very desirable environment for the fish or other creatures that may be selected by the user." The Fish Bath contains a freshwater source and an air-purification system for your denizens of the deep and is sealed against accidental soap infiltration. Its transparent design permits viewing of the aquarium from both the bathing position and from the outside of the tub. Sounds like fun, but we have a question: What kind of a view do the fish have?

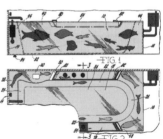

Super Trash Man

US Patent No. 4,854,003
Issue Date 1989

It's a bird! It's a plane! No, it's . . . it's . . . it's your neighbor with a trash bag strapped to his back! That's right folks, collecting garbage with a single stride, annihilating debris with every turn, he is—*Super Trash Man!* Complete with shoulder and feet harnesses, this working-class superhero's weapon was patented to help wipe out leaves and grass clippings with a single bound. Now you too can become a Super Trash Hero; you know, for the kids.

Underwater Rebreathing Mask

US Patent No. 2,477,706
Issue Date 1949

How long can you hold your breath? Would you like to do a little underwater sight-seeing but find bobbing to the surface for air every thirty seconds too annoying? Well, your prayers have been answered with the "Underwater Rebreathing Mask"! Patented in 1949, this invention provides a simple, inexpensive, lightweight, and leak-proof mask that allows you to "rebreath" your air underwater. The mask attaches to your face. A nose piece fits over your beak and contains passageways to the rebreathing bags mounted on the sides of your face. The eye holes are covered with glass for optimal visual pleasure. Just gulp some air while you're on the surface and

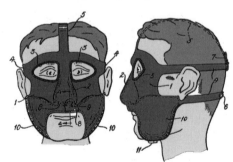

slip underwater. You need to breathe through your nose, into and out of the rebreathing bags. Enjoy the sights. Take your time, but eventually you will run out of air. The inventor suggests this will take about a minute and a half. Of special note from the inventor: Make sure to secure the chin strap (#11) to prevent the cheek bags from flapping and fluttering, and absolutely, positively, keep your mouth closed!

It's Alive!

Horse Diaper

US Patent No. 5,738,047
Issue Date 1998

Cleaning up after a horse can be a pain in the rear, so to speak. As the inventor tells us: "Frequent mucking-out of stables, horse-boxes, and like shelters and renewal of sawdust, etc., have in the past generally been necessary if the animal's accommodation is to be kept in reasonable condition. This can require copious labor of a tedious and unpleasant nature." His solution? Strap a big rubber diaper on your trusty steed! We call it a diaper, the inventor calls it an "Equidae Excrement Receptacle"

(Equidae: any of a family of perissodactyl mammals consisting of the horses, asses, zebras, and extinct related animals). Either way, if you think mucking is unpleasant work, try cleaning Trigger's diaper three times a day.

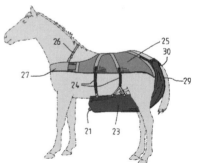

Duck Decoy and Blind Combo

US Patent No. 5,678,346
Issue Date 1997

Ducks can be very smart, so if you want to shoot a duck, you need to think like a duck. You have to crawl inside that duck's head and look around, see what makes him tick. *Be the duck!* Well, that's the only explanation we can come up with for this goofy-looking duck decoy/ blind. While it is a convenient way to haul your gun and food and beer to the duck pond, no self-respecting duck is going to come near this silly ensemble. Quack.

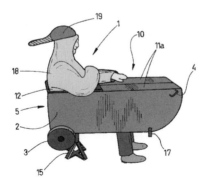

Dog Hoser

US Patent No. [3,771,192]
Issue Date [1973]

Good grooming is probably not on your dog's list of top priorities. In fact, if your dog even has a suspicion that a haircut is coming, he may perform a disappearing act that rivals the great Houdini! Professional groomers like to use a vacuum cleaner to remove clipped hair from the dog, but, according to the inventor, "these have not met with success because of the fear instilled in a dog at the sight of a vacuum cleaner and because of its very loud noise." The solution: the Dog Hoser, a hairy, dog-shaped shell with a vacuum cleaner in its belly and a retractable hose for a tail. After

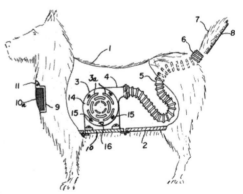

clipping your dog, introduce him to his new best friend. Then, confuse the heck out of Benji by proceeding to yank out the Hoser's tail and rub it all over him. Adding flea powder to the Hoser's tail allows you to combine two messy chores into one. The vacuum's muffled noise and the friendly shape make the Dog Hoser canine compatible, but your dog may never mate again.

It's Alive!

Cow Gas Gauge

US Patent No. 5,265,618
Issue Date 1993

Is the problem of trying to collect and measure gas emissions from livestock (or maybe your in-laws) keeping you awake at night? Have you ever wondered exactly how much energy cow burps emit? Now your curiosity can be satisfied with the 1973 patent of the "System for Measuring Metabolic Gas Emissions From Animals"! Designed to measure how much energy free-roaming livestock actually use, this device will help identify the feeding systems that allow the most efficient use of energy for the health of the cow. But wait! The device is fun and easy to use! First feed the subject a rubber tube, which acts as an internal tracer.

Attach the end of the tracer tube to the inflatable collar placed around the animal's neck. With every breath, metabolic gas samples are collected and analyzed. Hey, who said bovine belches weren't fun?

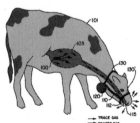

Mouse Puppet

US Patent No. [4,327,668]
Issue Date [1982]

We labeled this invention the Mouse Puppet, but the inventor calls it "a recreational device for providing coparticipatory activity for a pet owner and a pet." Wow, sounds like an attorney may have been involved. If you play mousy with your cat, you soon discover that Fur Ball is a carnivore and your hands are fair game. Biting and scratching are all part of the fun, and if you can't take the heat, get out of the hot tub (or something like that). Anyway, now you can coparticipate and keep all of your digits intact with the Mouse Puppet. Your hands operate the toy mice safely from below the fake mouse grass, and Fur Ball can be the terror that she imagines herself to be.

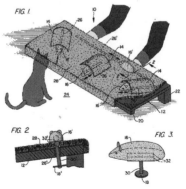

Dog Watch

US Patent No. 5,023,850
Issue Date 1991

The Dog Watch is actually a "clock for keeping time at a rate other than human time." Why would you need to know dog time? Beats the heck out of us, but with this handy watch, you can perceive time at your animal's rate instead of your own. How does it work? According to the inventor, the watch multiplies every human second, minute, and hour by seven, thus giving us "doggy time." If Fido lives to be the ripe old age of fourteen, that translates into ninety-eight human years! Or is that ninety-eight dog years?

Duck Shield

US Patent No. 5,572,823
Issue Date 1997

We're stumped by this patent. The *Absurd* staff has been discussing it for days, and we still don't know the answer. We just can't figure out who gets the "Dummy Award" for this patent. Are the ducks sooo stupid that if a hunter holds up a cheesy cutout, they will be duped into dropping anchor? Or is the hunter dumb enough to believe that the ducks really are that dumb? Or maybe the inventor should receive the "Bozo Award" for spending his hard-earned cash to patent this faux fowl? And we have to believe that by the time you drop your big bird silhouette and raise your gun to the skies, you will have scared off even the dullest of ducks.

Wig Flipper

US Patent No. 5,372,549
Issue Date 1994

Have you ever been so mad, you wanted to flip your wig? Well, now you can and without even causing your scalp grief. The concept of the Wig Flipper is simple: A wig (simulating your real hair) is placed on a large spring and attached to a small cap. The wig and spring are then compressed, locked onto the cap, and placed on your head. Now the real fun begins. Find your victim, push the release button, and your new hairpiece will jump up and dance in the air. We'll bet it would be even more entertaining on your shaggy dog.

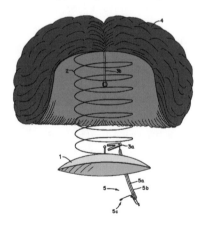

Ear Tubes

US Patent No. 4,233,942
Issue Date 1980

Does Fifi have dirty dog ears? Oh, you know she's your baby and so, so precious, but those big ears keep ending up in the food dish and it just ruins your lap time together. You *could* clean her ears, but they *are* very sensitive and she *is* seriously precious. So how can we make everyone happy? Ear Tubes! Because dogs don't care how silly they look. The Ear Tubes plastic ear-bondage system fits on Fifi like earmuffs with a chin strap. Might we add a suggestion? Next time you run out of toilet paper, cut the tube in half, cuff Princess's ears, and save yourself about thirty bucks.

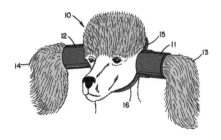

Fly Trap

US Patent No. 5,193,302
Issue Date 1993

Go ahead and admit it—you hate pesky houseflies. Flies are not welcome in most homes around the world, but how do you get rid of them? A big strand of sticky flypaper often works well, but it's very low on the visual-appeal charts. You could use one of those electric bug zappers in your kitchen, but the blue glow and searing popping sound can be annoying. Some people even resort to keeping carnivorous plants in the house, like the Venus flytrap. But what happens when the bug season dies down and your plant starts getting hungry? Now you're forced to go out and

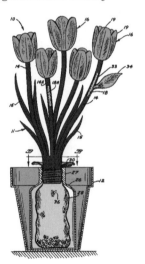

actually catch some flies to satisfy your plant's voracious urges. The world needed a better solution, and in 1993, the "Artificial Flower Fly Trap" came to our rescue. The idea is simple really: Artificial flowers are attached to hollow artificial stems. A fly attractant is placed in the blossoms and the stems of the trap. Once the bug enters the stem, it is trapped by thousands of microfilaments that point downward. The fly can walk down, but not out, and is captured in a convenient plastic bag concealed in the flowerpot. Just like the Roach Motel, "they can check in, but they can't check out."

It's Alive!

Flying Fish

US Patent No. 3,698,121
Issue Date 1972

Are you going on a fishing trip any time soon? Looking forward to trolling for fish on a yacht with nice weather, good food, and great friends, but dreading the laborious task of hauling your catch out of the water? Well, listen up, lazy, because this fishing apparatus invented in 1972 is your guarantee that you won't have to get out of your seat all day long! A gigantic balloon floats on the water surface above your baited hook. When you feel a pull on your line, press the button on your fishing pole and the balloon will

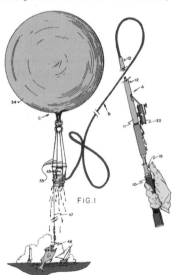

FIG.1

instantaneously fill with gas and hopefully hook your fish. You will watch in awe as your denizen of the deep is pulled effortlessly out of the water and suspended in midair. Now you can sit back and comfortably reel in your catch—*out of the air!* Better reel it in fast; seagulls may swoop in to devour your hanging fish (talk about the one that got away!).

It's Alive!

cranium cooler

FIG. 1

Chapter 3

all-terrain stroller

TOTALLY
ABSURD
INVENTIONS
America's Goofiest Patents

WEAR
THIS!

diaper alarm

5.125 in

25 in

FIG.1

FIG.2

US Patent No. 3,900,154
Issue Date 1975

Wear This!

Smoking while driving presents certain health risks. For example, a hot ash falling into your lap can have frightful consequences. How can you safely dispose of those pesky ashes? Never fear, the Big-Ash Bib is here! With this wacky invention, you can keep both hands securely on the steering wheel, because the cigarette never has to leave your mouth. To dispose of the cig's ashes, hum "Smoke Gets in Your Eyes," and wiggle your lips aggressively up and down until the ashes fall into

your Big-Ash Bib. We suggest placing the bib around your neck and wearing it everywhere. It's perfect for long business meetings, first dates, and watching *Wheel of Fortune*. Getting hungry? It's time to switch to the Car Bib (see page 72).

Extreme Comb Over

US Patent No. 4,022,227
Issue Date 1975

Unbelievable! Just when you think you've seen it all, something more incredible comes along. This is a patent for a three-way comb-over to cover a bald head. That's right, the U.S. Patent Office actually issued a patent for a method of combing your hair! The inventor was concerned for insolvent bald men that couldn't afford a bad hairpiece. Just let your hair grow long and goofy on the sides, then divide it into three sections and comb it over your bald head one section at a time. Be sure to add hair spray to each new hair layer. This may truly be the most totally absurd patent we have ever seen!

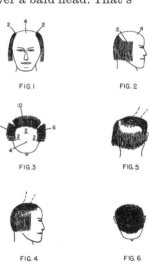

FIG. I

FIG. 2

FIG. 3

FIG. 5

FIG. 4

FIG. 6

US Patent No. 5,131,093
Issue Date 1992

Okay, admit it. It's a chore holding up your binoculars for long periods of time. But with the advent of the Bino Cap, not only will you be able to see up close and personal, but every patron at the opera will envy you. To use, simply whip out your folded paper Bino Cap, attach point A to point B, and so on, then slap on the cardboard binoculars via the Velcro fasteners. Sit back; enjoy the show; you're good to go! Not only will you have enhanced vision, but you will be creating quite a fashion statement as well. P.S. Just in case you were wondering, #103 is evidently a bad hair day. Hey, we all have them.

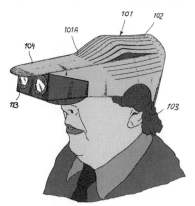

Wear This!

| Arm Mitten | US Patent No. 5,357,633 |
| | Issue Date 1994 |

In these modern times, garments are becoming more and more specialized, especially in the sporting domain. Clothes designed specifically for skiing, hiking, and biking have become commonplace. Top athletes such as professional baseball pitchers and football quarterbacks need special protection to keep their throwing arms in optimum condition. But the Arm Mitten wasn't designed to protect top athletes, my friend, oh no. Our inventor decided it was time to improve the lives of ordinary motorists like you and me. The Arm Mitten protects us from

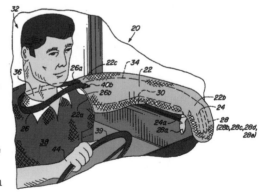

the devastating effects of highway-cruisin' sunburn. And it's about time! The inventor writes: "Air-conditioning is great, but driving on a lovely day with one's arm resting on the ledge of an open car window is found enjoyable by many drivers. The driver's enjoyment, however, can be shattered if the drive results in a severe sunburn to the hand or arm." You know it! So next time you decide to take a sunny drive, go crazy, lose the AC, roll down your window, and let the fresh air blow through your hair. But, hey, don't forget to wear protection! Make sure to slip into the singularly swank Arm Mitten.

Wear This!

Face Flexor

US Patent No. 4,666,148
Issue Date 1987

Have you looked in the mirror lately, concerned about gravity taking its toll? Are your facial features sagging a little too much, but plastic surgery just isn't for you? The answer to your problems may be the Face Flexor! This little exercise device is designed to firm up drooping facial flesh with quicker and better results than plain old regular facial exercises. To use the Face Flexor, just strap it on and squeeze the air pump several times. The inflatable vinyl lining of the mask will expand and press against your face, making facial exercises much more difficult. But not to worry, more resistance means shorter workouts. As an added bonus, you get the attached calorie counter and timer. Why not wear the Face Flexor while you eat lunch? It's like killing two birds with one stone. And, hey, your coworkers will have a scream.

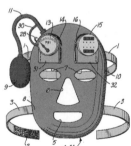

Bionic Exersuit

US Patent No. 5,820,534
Issue Date 1998

Are you tired of those bulky home-exercise devices that are taking up valuable space in your closet? Do you want to stay in shape, but going to the gym or hopping on a bicycle seems like toooo much effort? Well, fret no more. With the Bionic Exersuit, you can stay in shape by simply breathing! The Bionic Exersuit attaches to your legs, your shoulders, your feet, your arms, and everything in between. The suit works by providing resistance to any bodily movement. Every motion is met with resistance, making each gesture an exercise. So convenient, you can wear it all day. So attractive, you'll want to wear it all night.

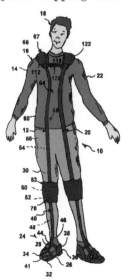

Birdman of Alcatraz

US Patent No. 5,996,127

Issue Date 1999

Bird-watching more and enjoying it less? Are you tired of using binoculars to get up close and personal with our flying friends? You need the Birdman of Alcatraz bird-feeding system, freshly patented for the new millennium. To attract hummingbirds and butterflies, fill the feeders (#107) with nectar and go sit in your favorite bird-watching spot. Your winged guests may be a bit nervous, so don't sneeze, cough, scratch, or twitch. Be sure to wear stylish mirrored aviator glasses to conceal prying eyes, and it wouldn't hurt to have brushed your

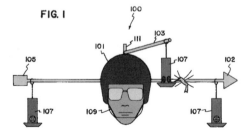

FIG. I

teeth before breathing on the birds. The inventor thought of everything! Number 213 is a counterweight and #215 is a perch/staging area for late-arriving birds waiting to gain access to the busy feeders. (A little optimistic, don't you think?) Number 217 is a magnifying glass and #100 is a dufus. If the flocks don't cooperate, stick some nuts in the feeders and let the squirrel fest begin!

Wear This!

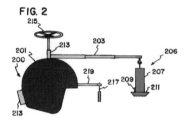

FIG. 2

Fingertip Toothbrush

US Patent No. 5,875,513
Issue Date 1999

Brushing more and enjoying it less? What you need is a novel approach, and we have just what the doctor, umm, dentist ordered. This handy little toothbrush is designed to give you more control and sensitivity when brushing your teeth. Since you have nerve endings in your fingertips (at least we hope you do), you can now feel your way around sensitive areas of your mouth. The rubbery, bushy thing on the tip of your finger connects to the elasticized handle so that, according to the inventor, "even the clumsier of persons" can hang on to this baby. You say you're not clumsy, just a bit sloppy? Never fear, the little circular bulge at the base of the handle is designed to keep saliva, water, and toothpaste from running down your wrist and into your sleeve. That's great news, except now what do you do with a palm full of foamy spittle?

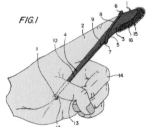

FIG.1

It's never too early to start your Christmas shopping. Why not be original this year and avoid the toys that everyone seems to be buying? Why not give the gift that keeps on giving, the "Apparatus for Aligning Image with Blind Spot of the Eye"! Patented in 1975, this toy allows the user to locate his blind spot! In order to play this amazingly fun game, strap the apparatus tightly on the top of your head. Close your left eye and focus on the dangling tab with your right eye, then switch eyes. Voilà! The dangling tab has disappeared into your blind spot. Not only will this invention provide endless hours of fun and good times for everyone (especially at parties), but anyone wearing it will unquestionably become irresistible to the opposite sex. Enjoy!

Wear This!

Boob Tube

US Patent No. 5,101,315
Issue Date 1992

Outdoor sporting events are a great way to enjoy fresh air and to cheer for your favorite team. But when the weather turns ugly, you need to protect yourself from the inclement elements.

Umbrellas are okay, but they block the view of the person behind you, and you still often end up getting wet. Not with the Boob Tube! This foul-weather suit is designed to protect you in rain, sleet, hail, or snow, while allowing a clear view for your fellow spectators. Now you can enjoy

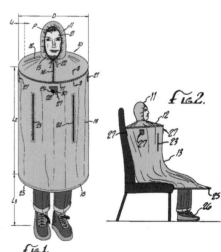

FIG.1.

FIG.2.

any event while snug and secure in your own little tube. For convenience, you get a couple of slits for your arms and a built-in hood. Fig. 2 demonstrates the ability to sit down and look like a tube of toothpaste. The inventor suggests that the Boob Tube can also be made of a reflective metal foil for protection against the sun, poisonous gases, or nuclear radiation. We suggest that when they drop the bomb, you'll end up looking like a giant burned Jiffy Pop.

Wear This!

Car Bib

US Patent No. 4,887,315
Issue Date 1989

Do you eat your favorite snacks while driving and drop messy morsels all over your shirt and lap? Food is flying all over the place, and you're more worried about getting a ketchup stain on your garb than watching the road ahead? Now what? If you were wearing this invention you could maintain clean clothes and a clean driving record!

The Car Bib was designed for the motorist that eats on the go, catching the chow that misses his mouth. The inventor notes that the device can also function as a serving tray for your eats. (Is that before or after the food has fallen from your mouth?)

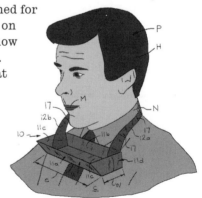

The upside of riding a motorcycle is the feeling of complete freedom. You can feel the wind in your hair as you ride, unencumbered by the confines of a car. But if you crash into something while cruising down the road, the bike stops and you are sent flying through the air. The downside of your complete freedom is Newton's Law of Gravity. What goes up, must come down. You will quickly come to a crashing, painful halt. But wait. . . . If you had strapped on your Crash Wings before embarking, our story could have had a happy ending. When you were ejected from the motorcycle, a parawing would have popped open and its lifting action would have glided you away from the crash site and floated you back to earth safely. Holy Batwing, Robin!

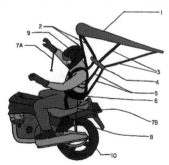

Wear This!

| Dance Fever |

US Patent No. 3,458,188
Issue Date 1969

Wear This!

Has your dance routine become old and tired? Do you desire a more tantalizing tango? This invention is the answer to dull dances and monotonous mambos! You and your partner simply adorn yourselves with this fancy dancing belt complete with flashing lights. Hey, don't forget to hook yourself up to your partner's waist so he can't run away when you step on his toes! Arthur Murray would be proud.

Kids need to get a grip. Well, at least when they are a tad on the wee side and still learning to eat with the proper mastication utensils (proper in Western cultures, anyway). Ever had a tot? If you had a penny (make that a dime) for every time you had to pick up that darn spoon and place it back in Junior's little wiggly hand, you could change your last name to Trump, no, make that Gates. But if you had the Spoon Truss, you would be a little poorer but far less weary, since the spoon is lashed to the wrist of the offender. Still got issues? Hey, no one said this invention would make him actually *use* the spoon.

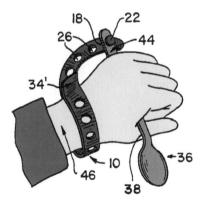

Ultimate Umbrella

US Patent No. 5,201,332
Issue Date 1993

The Ultimate Umbrella is either the world's largest baseball cap or the ugliest umbrella we've ever seen. The inventor's intent was to design a bigger and more stylish umbrella. Bigger to keep more of you dry; more stylish so you can be mo' chic, darling. For convenience, its head-mounted mechanism allows you to keep your hands free for thoughtful poses. But beware, where there's rain, there's lightning, and a well-placed jolt to this cranial lightning rod might just be what the doctor ordered . . . Dr. Frankenstein, that is!

Okay, we have a confession to make. This invention isn't really a bulletproof butt protector, but it is used to protect your backside. The butt guard is made of resilient, shock-absorbing plastic and foam and is secured at the waist with an adjustable belt. We're not sure if it was designed to prevent embarrassing buttock and hip injuries while skateboarding or designed to embarrass skateboarders with its delightful appearance. We have to question the riders' priorities here, there's no helmet to protect the brain bucket, but the butt is bound for bouncing.

Wear This!

Face Bake	US Patent No. 4,364,123
	Issue Date 1982

Summertime is beach time, and that means hauling your stuff from the car to the sand for fun in the sun. Let's see, there's the towel, the suntan lotion, a snack or two, and the beverage of your choice. Don't forget the snorkel, fins, and the shovel and bucket for building sand castles. Oh, and you gotta have your wireless phone. Beach time also means protecting yourself from sunburn and maybe catching an afternoon nap. So is there a product available that helps do all of these things? We're so glad you asked. Yes! The Face Bake is just such a

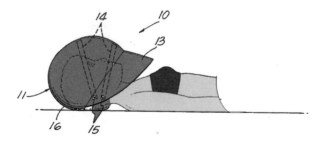

multipurpose device for all of your beach needs. You can toss all of your belongings into the molded-plastic scooplike thingy and haul them to the beach. Once you are firmly planted in the sand, you can place the Face Bake over your mug to protect yourself from the sun's powerful rays. Want to talk with friends? No problem, you can tilt the Face Bake upward and converse with friends while gulping for fresh air. And the Face Bake makes a superb seagull-fallout-prevention appliance.

Wear This!

Hat Tether

US Patent No. 5,675,841
Issue Date 1997

While some of our featured inventions have real practical applications, you just have to wonder who is actually going to use them. Take this next invention as an example. Losing your hat in the wind is an age-old problem. We'd even bet that's why chin straps were invented. But chin straps can be bothersome, and what self-respecting baseball cap wearer would put a chin strap on his hat? That brings us to the Hat Tether, practical yet goofy. The Hat Tether is a nylon cord that clips to the back of your shirt collar and the back of your hat. The wind blows, your hat flies off your head, and it dangles from your shirt collar. You don't lose your hat, and, heck, you could possibly even save your toupee with this gadget. One thing is for certain: The fashion police have already issued arrest warrants.

Long nails are all the fashion rage this year (in certain parts of Belarus, downwind of the Chernobyl power plant), and when it gets cold outside, it's hard to keep your well-manicured talons intact wearing traditional gloves. But with Scary Fingers, you can keep your digits warm and toasty while flashing your Lee press-ons to the world! The trick is to fit regular gloves with little elastic rings that allow your nails to poke through and enjoy the freedom they deserve. You say you don't live in Belarus? Not to worry, buy a pair for your nail-biting friends; they can chew away like mad beavers and never harm their lovely new gloves.

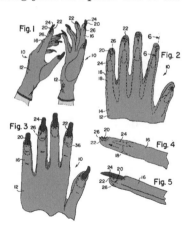

Snowboarder Bumper

US Patent No. 6,019,608
Issue Date 2000

Learning to snowboard can be difficult. The subtle twists and turns necessary to control a snowboard can get lost in the chaos of merely staying upright. Falling down is all part of the learning process, even for accomplished skiers. So how do you keep from hurting yourself while you're still in the klutz phase of training? The Snowboarder Bumper! This handy little device fits most snowboarders and is worn like a vest, only bigger, much bigger. When you

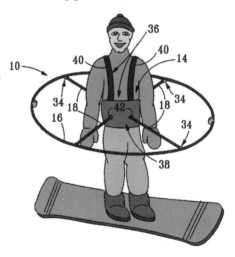

start to fall down, the Snowboarder Bumper will keep you upright enough to recover your balance quickly and easily. Trees getting in your way? No problem—you'll just bounce right off. If you do manage to fall down, you may just become the world's largest living snowball. Helpful hint: Don't forget to remove your bumper before attempting to enter the lodge.

Wear This!

Marilyn Manson Exercise Suit

US Patent No. 5,820,530
Issue Date 1998

Forget jogging; forget hiking; forget swimming. If you really want to get a great workout, you need the Marilyn Manson Exercise Suit. Those other activities can jar your body or provide incomplete workouts. But the MMES is designed for optimal biomechanical exertion positioning. To use, don the suit, jump into the nearest swimming pool, and fiddle about. Of course you'll need about five assistants to help you get into this ensemble and you'll be exhausted just from blowing up all the air bags, but, hey, it looks good *and* it's good for you!

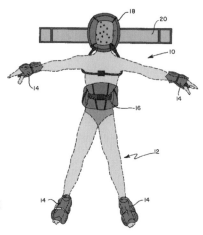

Keg Head	US Patent No. 5,966,743
	Issue Date 1999

Do you yearn to be the life of the party, the person that everyone wants to hang out with? Is being the center of attention your deepest desire? If so, then you need the Keg Head! This new indispensable dispenser of your favorite beverage is part hat and part keg, combined for your pleasure. Once the party begins, prepare to position yourself near the front door, so you can greet thirsty guests with a big smile and a cool, quenching refreshment. Not for the timid, the Keg Head will keep you encircled with a parched party population all night long. But don't let that go to your head. They aren't there to get to know the inner you; it's the beer, stupid!

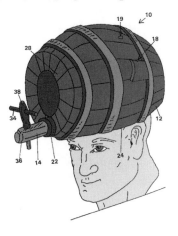

Wear This!

Picture yourself at a baseball game, sitting in the sun on a warm day, tan and relaxed, when all of a sudden a pop fly is whacked your way. What to do? Do you (a) duck and let the more alert fans deal with it, (b) try to catch it bare handed, (c) sit still and hope it misses you? Answer: (d) Nonchalantly remove your Mitt Cap, insert your digits into the finger panel, and make a flawless catch, amazing your friends and neighboring fans. Every baseball fan needs one, and with the odds of the lottery, you may someday actually get to use it.

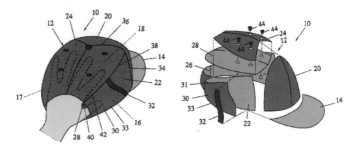

Rain Dome

US Patent No. 5,978,967
Issue Date 1999

Rain, rain, go away, come back another . . . Okay, that's not working; guess it's time to break out the Rain Dome! This chic plastic "cone of silence" is designed to store flat and pop open the instant you feel a raindrop. Convenient air vents allow fresh air in and keep rain out. The Rain Dome's best feature (besides its obvious elegance) is a hair pouch (#28) to keep ponytails and long hair dry. It looks to us like guys with long beards can simply turn the dome around and tuck their beard into the pouch. (Are you listening, ZZ Top?) The dome can also come in handy during food fights and up-close bird-watching.

Wear This!

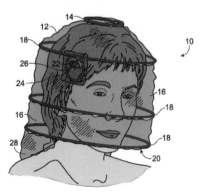

Nose Wipe

US Patent No. 4,536,889
Issue Date 1985

This fine invention is best summed up by a lengthy quote from the inventor. "Nose drip is a very frequent accompaniment to the cold-weather outdoor activity of skiing. This requires frequent wiping of the nose and/or face by facial tissues or the like. Heretofore, a skier with irritating nose drip has generally found it necessary to stop, disengage at least one pole and one ski glove, retrieve tissues, handkerchief, or the like from a pocket, use it, and return it to the pocket for later disposal. This troublesome sequence often leads skiers, especially children, to use such wiping expedients as the sleeves of the jacket, to avoid such

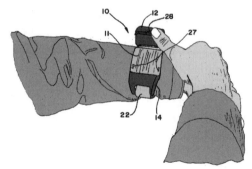

trouble, bother, interruption, and delay. This solution is generally unattractive to older skiers, and also to the parents of said children. Often, rather than interrupt the ski run, the skier endures the irritation of the nose drip until the run is over, a solution which can take a considerable amount of enjoyment out of recreational skiing." The Nose Wipe, snot a bad idea!

Wear This!

Panty Hose x 3

US Patent No. 5,713,081
Issue Date 1997

Are these crazy panty hose designed for a cloning experiment gone wrong? No, they're a somewhat practical yet goofy-looking solution to an age-old problem. Ladies, you know what we mean—the dilemma of unsightly runs in your panty hose. With Panty Hose x 3, you don't have to carry a spare and chuck the old pair when you get a run or hole in your panty hose. With this ingenious design, you simply (and discretely) rotate your leg into the new, unblemished panty hose appendage. The damaged hosiery leg is then tucked into a pocket in the crotch of the panty hose. Comfortable? You be the judge.

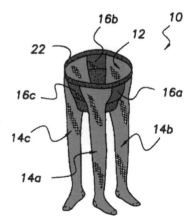

Sled Pants

US Patent No. 5,573,256
Issue Date 1996

Snowboarding is all the rage. Surfing down the slopes is a great way to enjoy the snow and look cool. But what if you're a bit of a klutz and just can't keep your balance on a snowboard? Is it still possible to have some winter fun and be a babe magnet? If you are wearing these Sled Pants, then the answer is an emphatic yes! The Sled Pants are ergonomically engineered to fit your posterior. When you're ready to hit the slopes, simply reach behind you and fold down the leg-support portion of your pants. Aim yourself downhill and be seated. Oh, and make sure you wear your Sled Pants when you strut your stuff at the ski lodge.

Wear This!

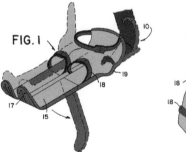

FIG. 1

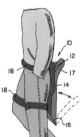

Cranium Cooler

US Patent No. 4,551,857
Issue Date 1985

Does your hat's hot, sweaty headband press against your forehead and cause you to overheat on a scorching summer day? Are you tired of wearing plain old hats that offer only shade or perhaps respite from a bad hair day? Well, hang on to your hats, folks, because summer-heat relief is on its way! The Cranium Cooler offers soothing heat relief by converting solar energy into a very cool forehead chiller. The concept is really quite simple. The solar cells on the hat gather the sun's energy. This energy is transferred to a Peltier-effect thermoelectric device that cools the wearer's forehead. A little radiator is mounted on the front to dissipate excess heat. Deep down, we actually like this invention's concept. But, unless you dangle lots of little furry balls from the brim and become a flamenco dancer, we're afraid the fashion police will be issuing citations.

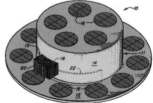

Twist and Shout

US Patent No. 6,013,013
Issue Date 2000

We don't know about you, but if we're going to exercise, it has to be fun and fairly easy. Instead, we introduce you to an apparent torture device we aptly call the Twist and Shout. The T&S is designed to help improve your golf swing by strengthening your swinging muscles through elastic resistance. When worn, the device is supposed to emulate your golf stance and can even simulate an uneven lie. Religious symbolism be damned, it's time to play your favorite Chubby Checker CD and twist the night away.

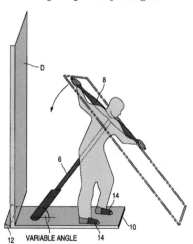

93 · Totally Absurd Inventions

Hospital Happiness

US Patent No. 6,012,168
Issue Date 2000

Ever feel exposed to the world when you wear a hospital gown? Our inventor says, "As most medical patients are all too acutely aware, all hospital-style gowns have rear openings seemingly designed to maximize the potential for embarrassment due to the virtually unavoidable exposure of the patient's buttock area while wearing such a gown." Ahem, well said. We say, "Cleavage be gone with the new Hospital Happiness modesty flap!" Freshly patented for the new millennium, patients can now easily avoid embarrassing medical moments, while doctors and nurses performing procedures can simply flip the flap.

While we make fun of this unflappable attire, we will be the first in line to request our own Hospital Happiness.

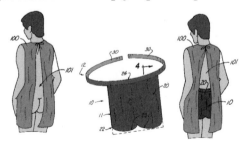

Chapter 4

IT'S MOVING!

Low-ratio four-wheel drive, ultra-traction balloon tires, lift-kit ground clearance system—these options assure that your sport utility vehicle can go off-road to where the action is. Never mind the fact that most SUVs are used to haul the kids, the dog, and the groceries on a nice paved road, you gotta *look* like you can go anywhere. Well, now you can go anywhere with the super-duper Monster Truck tracked-vehicle conversion kit. Great for mud, snow, rocks, bigger rocks, and driving over parked cars, with the Monster Truck kit, you'll never get stuck again. Step ladder not included.

It's Moving!

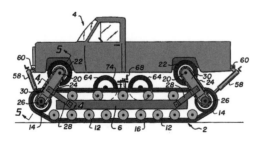

It's Moving!

The skating sensation of the 1990s, the Rollerblade, was perhaps inspired by this invention of the 1970s. The single-wheel roller skate was conceived to transform old-fashioned four-wheel roller skating into a new and exciting phenomenon. The concept: to improve roller skating by making it more challenging and skillful. The problem: only one wheel. Sadly, this invention never got rolling.

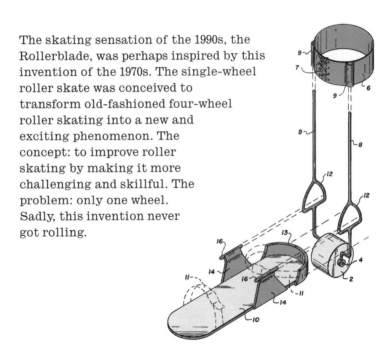

Ski Fan

US Patent No. 4,189,019
Issue Date 1980

Have you heard about the newest winter Olympic event, uphill skiing? Interested in snow skiing, but you don't have any hills or mountains nearby, not to mention the energy required to swoosh all day long? Now you can actually ski and relax at the same time with the gas-powered Ski Fan. This invention straps onto your back and is steered by hand controls. The peaceful solitude usually associated with skiing may be lacking here (think your lawn mower is noisy?), and don't even ask about the brakes.

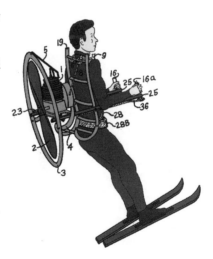

It's Moving!

Knee Skates

US Patent No. 5,725,224
Issue Date 1998

Skating has been around for years, and with the popularity of in-line skates, it seems like everyone is rolling around. Our inventor likes to skate, but he had a little problem. When he stopped rolling long enough for a bite to eat or to do some shopping, he wasn't allowed in the stores because of his skates. He could carry some shoes with him and change, but he's a man in a hurry and didn't want to be bothered with this tiresome task—so he invented Knee Skates. This new method of skating allows you to boogie on

down the road in style. You have a couple of steering sticks for directional control and some nice leather pads on your toes allowing you to stop most of the time. But the inventor's biggest thrill of all, he can now stop skating, stand up, and immediately walk on his own two shoes, and he's welcome anywhere they allow goofballs.

It's Moving!

All Terrain Stroller

US Patent No. 2,422,254
Issue Date 1947

Do you sometimes feel that city environments are a little too harsh for your baby? How do you deal with pushy crowds, broken sidewalks, and curbs that must be circumvented at every corner? Well, we have the answer for all of you urban warriors out there, the ATS (All Terrain Stroller). Stick your little bambino in this torpedo with tank tracks and he will experience a smooth, quiet ride, gliding over virtually any surface, no matter how rough. There's even a convenient hand brake on the ATS, just in case you mow down a slow pedestrian!

So, you're all grown up and you still don't know how to roller skate? The Western Skater will give you the support and confidence you need to take that giant first step. As the inventor puts it, "The vehicle permits a beginner skater to train in a relatively uninhibited manner. . . ." We think you would have to be pretty uninhibited to get on this hobby horse in public. Now you can become the cowboy on roller skates you always dreamed of as a kid! Two words sum up this goofy-looking patent: *Giddy up!*

Fig.1

It's Moving!

Quad Power

US Patent No. 5,785,336
Issue Date 1998

How many gears do you have on your bicycle? One? Ten? Twenty-one? You could slap as many gears on there as you'd like, but you'd still have only two legs (we hope). What you need for those steep hills is more muscle power, and we're not talking a bicycle built for two, we're talking arm power! That's right, time to flex those biceps and triceps and flap your wings as you mow down those mountains and turn them into mole hills. Keep loose clothing and babies away from that dangerous-looking steering-gear mess (did OSHA approve this thing?). The Quad Power is more complex than a 747, so if you can't walk and chew gum at the same time, stay off this thing!

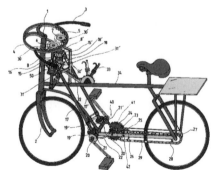

Snow season is in full swing (somewhere in the world), and it's time to break the mold and try something new. Some of us like to ski and some of us like to snowmobile. The inventor sums it up best: "The purists use nothing but skis, while the modernists take their relaxation along with their recreation and mount a snowmobile." We say: Bust the serene peace and quiet of Mother Nature wide open with your ear-piercing, chainsaw-motor-driven, poor-man's snowmobile, the Ultra Ski. Have fun, pop a wheelie, or tow your friends while your index finger is getting a full-digit workout operating the throttle (#29). But wait, there's more. Weary skiers can disengage the Ultra Ski and rev the chainsaw motor on their backs (#16) for a soothing, vibrating massage. Then call their chiropractor.

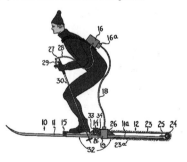

It's Moving!

Windmill Boat

US Patent No. 4,276,033
Issue Date 1981

Lack of wind can sure put a damper on the sport of sailing. Wind is unpredictable, so some sailboats carry gas-powered motors. However, fuel is not cheap and causes pollution. So what is an environmentally correct skipper to do? How about taking a three-hour tour in Windmill Boat! The amazing Windmill Boat has an umbrella-shaped sail that slowly rotates to propel the boat and generate electricity. The electricity generated is then stored in batteries for later use and can be used to power your cabin appliances as well. Hey, Professor, you will eliminate air and water pollution at the same time! The most absurd thing of all, when positioned straight up, the sail can serve as a gigantic parasol to shade Ginger and Marianne from the sun. No kidding?

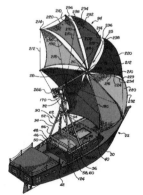

Foot Hoops

US Patent No. 4,363,493
Issue Date 1982

If you've ever donned in-line skates, you know that skating over a pebble can seem like hitting a boulder. On a rough surface, those small skate wheels vibrate so much, it can make your teeth rattle, so the inventor thought big and designed Foot Hoops. Bigger tires give a smoother ride, and you get to wear nifty shin braces too. Need skating instructions? The inventor explains everything in this quote from his patent. "The propulsive force is generated by allowing the loaded foot to veer off the outside of the travel path while the rider falls onto the other foot and at the final instant of fall, strokes vigorously. The magnitude of the forward force vector component depends on the angular divergence of the track of the loaded foot from the travel path and the vigor of the final stroke." Hmmmm. One last word of caution: Baggy pants could be your downfall.

It's Moving!

Senseless Scooter

US Patent No. 5,163,696
Issue Date 1992

Scooters are an age-old mode of transportation and fun for kids worldwide. Typically, you leave one foot on the scooter and push off from the ground with your other foot for locomotion. Sounds simple enough, but our inventor had a better idea, or so he thought. His idea was to add a flywheel to the scooter. A flywheel is a heavy rotating wheel that stores energy. The concept: By using a flywheel, you can get your scooter revved up and then jump on for a longer ride. To power your flywheel, the Senseless Scooter utilizes a spring-loaded drive mechanism that requires you to push down on the riding platform.

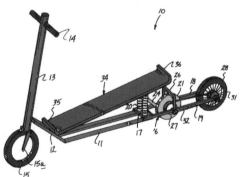

The problem: How in the heck are you supposed to get this thing going? For the life of us, we can't figure it out. Do you stand on the scooter and jump up and down, or do you run alongside of it and jump on and off? Either way, this is a totally Senseless Scooter. How does that saying go? If it ain't broke, don't fix it!

It's Moving!

Boat Ball

US Patent No. 3,933,115
Issue Date 1976

Every once in a great while, someone will reinvent the way we think of everyday objects. This inventor had a truly unique vision of how a boat could look and operate. Introducing the Boat Ball! Unlike your everyday boat that drags through the water, this motorized ball floats over the surface. The result: higher speeds and lower fuel consumption. The airplanelike passenger cabins are mounted on the sides of the monstrous ball and remain horizontal as the boat rolls ahead. In the event of a Titanic-type mishap, the watertight cabins can be released from the rotund mother ship and sail on their merry way.

Skate Scooter	US Patent No. 4,456,089
	Issue Date 1984

We can't figure out if this is the world's most inexpensive motorized vehicle or just a lazy person's way of getting some fresh air. The Skate Scooter is simply a motor attached to a wheel, with a throttle for speed control and a brake. The inventor says the Skate Scooter is "a driving vehicle by which the skater may enjoy skating by being pulled or pushed." We would like to caution riders that are being pushed to heed all speed-bump warning signs.

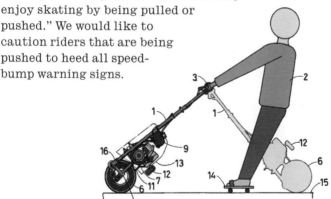

Golf Wand

US Patent No. 5,785,603
Issue Date 1998

Is your stance correct? Is your backswing correctly pendulant? Do you mind looking ridiculous? If you need practical guidance to execute a proper swing and the golf pro has given up on you, get yourself a Golf Wand swing aid. The key ingredient in developing a successful backswing is the appropriate amount of rotation of the

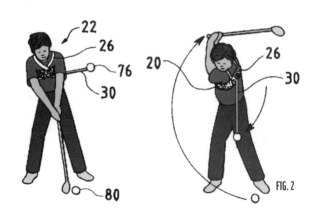

FIG. 1

FIG. 2

torso and back. So how can this swinging invention help you become the next Tiger Woods? Here's the theory: To develop the correct backswing, the ball on the end of the wand (#76, hereupon referred to as the wand ball) should be pointed in the general direction of your shot (fig. 1). If your backswing is in the correct position, the wand ball should line up between your eyeballs and the golf ball (fig. 2). Now you're good to go. . . . Fore! Potential invention design flaw: Before you arrive at fig. 2, we suggest wearing a protective cup.

It's Moving!

Windy Wheels

US Patent No. 4,735,429
Issue Date 1988

Sick of pedaling your bicycle but like the fresh air? Harness the power of the wind and sail like an ancient mariner on your wacky and wonderful Windy Wheels. Just hop on the bike and head on down the road. If there is sufficient wind, the self-adjusting sail will speed you on your merry way. Going upwind? Sailors tack from side to side, but that can be risky on a busy street or narrow sidewalk. Need to stop quickly during a strong gust of wind? Find something big and ram it.

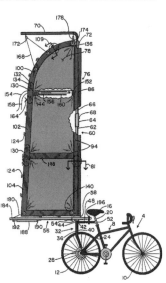

Robo Skater

US Patent No. 5,926,857
Issue Date 1999

What has twenty-six wheels, looks like Robocop, and can roll around on his rear end? It's Robo Skater! He has wheels on his feet, his toes, his elbows, his rear, his back, his chest, and even his hands. What, no wheels on his ears? Designed for a new, as of yet unnamed, sport, the Robo Skater assures the participant of a full-body workout. With this festive new rolling armor, you can skate lying down, on your knees, your tush, and all points in between. Fig. 2g even illustrates how to land swim. As a bonus, couch potatoes can walk their big dogs while simulating lying on the sofa (Fig. 2k). Mush, Fido! Missing essential component? Brakes!

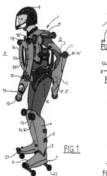

FIG.1

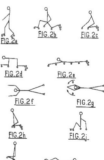

FIG.2a FIG.2b FIG.2c FIG.2d FIG.2e FIG.2f FIG.2g FIG.2h FIG.2j FIG.2i FIG.2k

Inchworm	US Patent No. [3,900,076]
	Issue Date [1975]

Check it out. Sit down in this two-legged dune buggy, pull back on the hand lever, and it rears up on its hind leg (#14), and if all goes according to plan, it won't fall over. To stay erect, the Inchworm is balanced by a couple of gyroscopes and gimbals and is powered by a small, caboose-shaped motor (#70). Next, push the lever forward and the front leg (#12) extends ahead, allowing the Inchworm to carefully lower itself onto both legs. Why create such an ungainly walking machine? you might ask. The inventor believes this type of

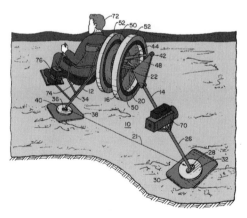

transport is superior to military tanks for traversing certain rough terrain and marshy marshes. Our question of the day: Who's going to use an Inchworm? If you are wheelchair bound, then the Inchworm could take you to exciting locales, but it's one very expensive mode of transportation. If you have full use of your legs, we say use them! Get off your idle bum and walk. What's the cost of the Inchworm? Let's see, if the U.S. government is paying $600 for mere toilet seats, this little larva-imitating chariot should cost about fifty zillion dollars.

It's Moving!

Mother of All Skateboards

US Patent No. 6,007,074

Issue Date 1999

Skateboarding can be hazardous with curbs and cracks and bumps everywhere. And while a fun part of skateboarding is overcoming these impediments by jumping them, crashing is the un-fun part. But now, with the Mother of All Skateboards, nothing can stop you! Obstacles, schmobstacles, we eat obstacles with this thing! This mother is loaded with cool features. It has an undivided continuous-axle differential transmission drive, and from the sound of it, that must be important. The MOAS is completely controlled with your toes and heels by pressing and twisting the skate pedals. You can control skating forward and backward, accelerate, decelerate, free-run, brake, and turn right or left. Curbs, we don't heed no stinkin' curbs!

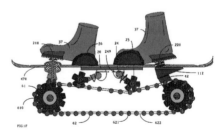

FIG.1F

Golf Schwing

US Patent No. 5,242,344
Issue Date 1993

Abdomenizer, Thighmaster, Face Flexor—wow, there's a piece of exercise equipment for just about everything. But our intrepid inventor thought maybe we could use just one more. You see, the problem with other golf gear is that it may help you improve your form, but it won't make you any stronger, hence the Golf Schwing. Golf not your game? The inventor says this wonderful piece of swing silliness can be modified to improve your polo stroke. We think the horse may get tired of hanging out in your weight room.

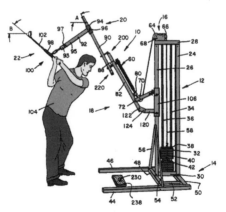

Roller Putter

US Patent No. 5,207,721
Issue Date 1993

Golf is a very complex sport, and mastering the putting greens can be maddening. Tapping that little ball just right requires years of practice, and that can wear you down. But the lazy man's golf game has been taken to new heights with the invention of the Roller Putter. The RP has a couple of turf-gripping wheels to ease it along the greens, so your arms and back can remain in good condition for the twelve-ounce lifts following the game. And it's not just your everyday

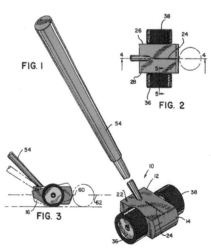

FIG. 1

FIG. 2

FIG. 3

It's Moving!

putter with some wheels on it, my friend, oh no. The inventor put a lot of time and thought into this little ping machine. We quote: "the head having a ball striking surface generally orthogonal to the upper surface and having a convex radius thereon such that the same portion of the ball is contacted independently of the angle of the shaft and the head." If you understand that, pass "Go" and head straight to the 19th hole, we're buyin'.

It's Moving!

Motorized Ice Cream Cone

US Patent No. 5,971,829
Issue Date 1999

I scream; you scream; we all scream for ice cream! How do you like to eat your ice cream? Our inventor says the old boring way is when "ice cream is gradually consumed through repeated licking actions of the person's tongue."

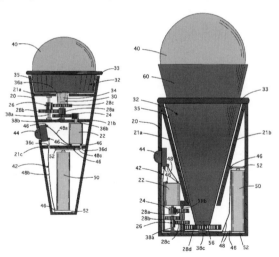

That is, until now! Introducing the Motorized Ice Cream Cone, designed to delight any child or the inner child within your tongue. We like the concept here. To fire this baby up, just push the handy ON/OFF switch on the side of the cone. Your ice cream will spin round and round as your tongue makes wonderful designs while slurping your summertime dairy dessert. Or, as our inventor explains, "it expands the typical act of eating an ice cream cone to include numerous playful and creative possibilities, including sculpting and carving of channels with one's tongue to form interesting shapes and patterns on the outer surface of an ice cream portion." In other words, it's okay to play with your food. Typically the Motorized Ice Cream Cone spins, but it can also rotate, vibrate, and agitate. We just hope it has a speed control, or you'll be wearing your triple cookie dough fudge mocha.

It's Moving!

It's Moving!

What do you get when you combine a pogo stick, a unicycle, and ugly boots? Pogo Shoes! These hazardous wonders were designed for fun and diversion. The diversion could very well be a trip to the hospital. To start your fun, the inventor suggests you get up (we haven't figured out how yet) and "urge your weight up and down until you bounce clear of the ground." Now about that landing . . . These things should be sold with crutches and Bulletproof Buttocks (see page 77). And the best news yet: no brakes!

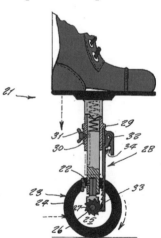

cranium cooler

FIG. 1

Chapter 5

all-terrain stroller

SHOCKING!

diaper alarm

US Patent No. 5,787,895
Issue Date 1998

If you enjoy kisses but dread the idea of getting a disease, then the Kissing Shield is a "must have" item. This germ barrier consists of a thin latex membrane artfully stretched over an attractive and romantic heart-shaped frame. The inventor states the shield is for kissing the intended recipient of the user's affection and is also useful for politicians when kissing babies. Hey, they got our vote.

Shocking!

Is Benji cooped up all day in your apartment and dying to see you so he can finally get some relief? Or are you tired of scooping that unsightly and ever odorous cat litter day after day after day? Worries be gone with the new and improved Pet Toilet! This little beauty patented in 1980 can solve your problems and give Benji and Fluffy their bathroom independence as well. An elegant ramp leads to the pet commode, which rests conveniently atop a conventional toilet. After your pet does its daily duty, a sensing device detects that your pet has been

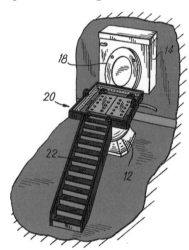

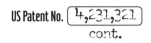
on and has departed from the trapdoor. The commode then automatically flushes water from the perforated tube surrounding the perimeter. Fluffy's entertainment now begins as the trapdoor flies open and, presto—waste be gone! This accessory is sure to be a delight for any pet as long as it doesn't exceed the weight limit on the trapdoor (fat cats need not apply).

Shocking!

This apparatus was patented in 1930 as a crime-fighting tool. The "Criminal Truth Extractor" was used to induce admissions of guilt by means of a frightening apparition: a skeleton with blinking eyes and a translucent astral body. Amid this supernatural atmosphere, an examiner in an adjoining room would ask questions and the suspect's replies and expressions would be recorded by camera and taped for later use. Yeah, that skeleton is pretty scary.

Shocking!

Bumper Dumper

US Patent No. 6,023,792
Issue Date 2000

Camping can lack certain niceties we have all come to appreciate, such as a place to sit and ponder yonder while our daily duties grow fonder (we're not exactly sure what this means, but we really wanted it to rhyme). If you're tired of using the bushes or smelly outhouses, here's your dream come true, the Bumper Dumper. Just plug it into the trailer hitch of your vehicle (we'd like to think it's a pick'emup truck) and have at it. We're not sure how intimate you want to be with your friends and neighbors, but a Bumper Dumper portable privacy screen would be a nice accessory.

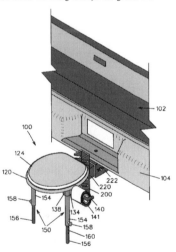

Shocking!

In today's health-conscious age, gardening and growing your own vegetables has become commonplace. If you are tired of your produce looking exactly like your neighbor's, then this mold was made just for you! This invention allows vegetables to grow into a wide variety of astonishing configurations and desired fanciful shapes, including the human head! Don't worry, the details of hair, eyebrows, nose, and mouth are reproduced with

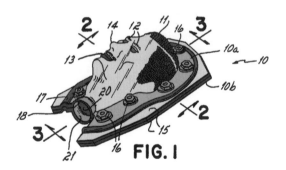

FIG. 1

Shocking!

amazing accuracy. There are no special growing
conditions required for your produce. Simply place the
growing vegetable inside the transparent mold.
Ultimately the vegetable expands so that it completely
fills the entire mold cavity. Soon you will have a
Sylvester Stallone squash, a David Hasselhoff zucchini,
or a Mel Gibson gourd head. Just think of the
compliments you will receive at your next dinner party
when you serve a pumpkin in the shape of Ozzy
Osbourne's head! Talk about a delicacy.

Shocking!

Have you ever gotten something stuck in your eye, and you can't find it, but it feels like a boulder, and you know if you don't get rid of it right now, you're going to go crazy? Our eyes are very sensitive, and even the smallest foreign object can really, really hurt. You may end up going to the doctor, and to help with your examination, the doctor may apply the Eyelash Retractor! Ahhhhh, run for your lives, this thing looks scary! Invented by the Marquis de Sade, the Eyelash Retractor can also be used for eye surgery, horror movies, and Halloween parties.

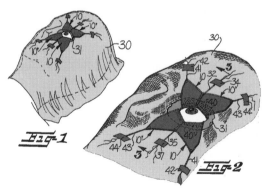

Shocking!

When small kids see a needle, they often go ballistic. Big tears, screams of terror, and some of the saddest faces on the planet. And who can blame them? They know pain is going to pay a visit and that their only hope is to delay the agony. The Bunny Syringe was invented to ease the inevitable for the kid and the doctor. The syringe is disguised as a cute bunny with a big smile and a very long, thin nose. Hopefully, by the time Mr. Bunny bites into Junior's rear, he won't know what hit him. Our concern is for the now-besmirched reputation of bunnies everywhere, not to mention the years of psychotherapy Junior will need to overcome his fear of floppy-eared rodents.

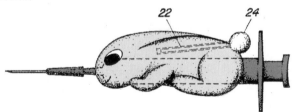

Shocking!

Motorcycle Air Bag

US Patent No. 4,825,469
Issue Date 1989

Although it may look like a Martian bodysuit, this is really fashionable inflatable motorcycle wear. The giveaway here is the bungee cord strapped to our hooded hero's waist. This protective air bag is designed to cushion the rider's fall during an accident. When forcefully ejected from the bike (yes, #36 is supposed to be a wall), the suit swells with compressed gas until it covers head, arms, torso, and legs but not, apparently, the fingertips. Heck, it's hard enough to pass helmet laws, let alone fashion laws. Evel Knievel Jr. wouldn't be caught injured in this thing.

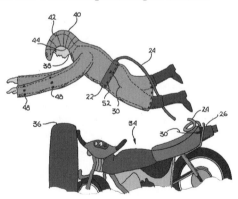

Two questions: (1) Ever wish you had a way to harness your youngster's boundless energy? (2) Do you hate mowing the lawn and view it as a necessary chore needed to keep your little jungle at bay? If you answered yes to both questions, we have the solution, the Tricycle Lawn Mower. This invention is definitely going to give the Children's Safety Council nightmares, but we can only imagine the compliments you will receive on your lawn.

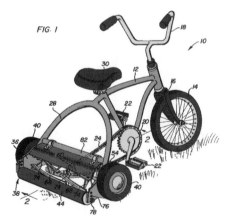

FIG. 1

Shocking!

Hair loss can be devastating. Baldness can cause lack of self-esteem and make you look years older. So every year, zillions of dollars are spent on hair-restoring products and devices. Now you can stop pulling your hair out looking for a naked-head solution, because we've found a surefire way to restore hair. It's called the Hot Head, and the idea behind it is simple: Steam your head clean, add restorer, and squish it into your scalp with highly compressed air.

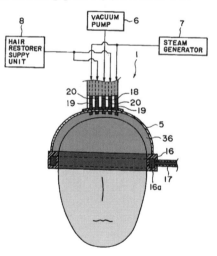

Shocking!

That's right, we said steam your head! To use the Hot Head, fire up your steam generator, pop on your steam helmet, making sure the sealing ring is on tight, then open the valve and sit back and relax, that is, if you can. Hot steam is jetted through the inlet metal pipes to the Hot Head and then into your scalp. There's no need to sweat the details, because the Hot Head is completely automatic. Next, restorer is sprayed onto your unadorned dome and then highly compressed air forces restorer into your scalp via the Hot Head pneumatic compressor. Some people have argued that this thing will never work, so let's just hope cooler heads prevail.

Shocking!

Portable Nuclear Shelter

US Patent No. 4,625,468
Issue Date 1986

You say you need significant life-saving protection from airborne radioactive fallout? Is the cost of construction and maintenance keeping you from enjoying the comforts of a permanent fallout shelter? Now your worries are over! When the "Big A" hits, simply dig a hole in the ground and erect this portable fallout shelter. It's equipped with a built-in water supply and an air-filtration system that is activated by flapping the sides of the tent. Patented in 1983 so that you too can be gamma safe and penny wise.

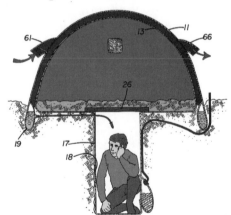

Shocking!

Picture, if you will, a warm summer evening, Kansas City, 1965. Okay, we're having a tough time visualizing that too. But apparently there was some trash burning going on in KC, where they know and love barbeque. So the inventor's lightbulb went on and the "Combined Trash Burner and Barbecue Pit" was born unto this world. Let us give you a tour. The burgers and ribs cook on #8, the grate. Charcoal and trash share #7 (hopefully, not at the same time), and all ashes land below. Best news yet: From a design standpoint, the inventor says it provides "a pleasing sight when placed in one's backyard or the like." We couldn't agree more.

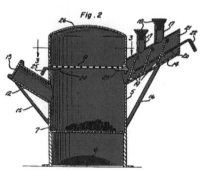

Fig. 2

Shocking!

A problem with chewing tobacco is spitting, a lot of spitting. The solution: a Portable Spittoon patented in 1983. With it, you can chew and spit tobacco, anywhere you please! No more back porches for you, buddy! Don't worry about your friends being revolted by your new habit either; at dinnertime, they'll appreciate your hiding your spittoon on the floor under the table. Better than using their good china, right? The spittle receptacle can clip right onto your favorite armchair, making it perfect for watching the game—work up a good gob and just sputter into the funnel. Bring it on a date in its convenient carrying case; it makes a great conversation piece. "Wanna see how much I spit all evening?"

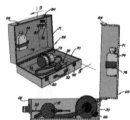

US Patent No. 5,652,959
Issue Date 1996

Finally, a hat designed for the ultimate fan. Now you can burn your favorite team logo right into your forehead! The skin stencil is a cutout design in the headband of your hat. The area around the cutout stencil blocks ultraviolet radiation from reaching your skin, resulting in your favorite team slogan tanning into and onto your forehead! We suggest that you don't apply any sunblock to your forehead and stay in the hot sun all day so tomorrow will truly be a red-letter day! (This suggestion is not endorsed by the National Cancer Institute.)

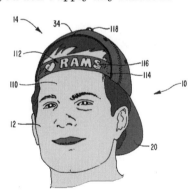

Shocking!

Junior Jail

US Patent No. 4,205,669
Issue Date 1980

Our inventor had probably changed one too many diapers the day this invention came to mind. It's designed to aid in diaper changing and cleaning up the aftermath. Sure, little legs and hands can flail and kick, and a full-body wiggle doesn't make things any easier, but putting Junior in restraints seems a bit extreme. To use, simply place baby on his back, secure the torso barrier, and strap in those cute little fluttering feet. Now take your time, relax: Junior isn't going anywhere.

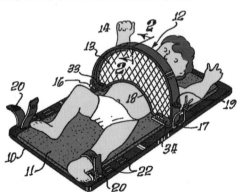

Shocking!

If you want your hair braided and there's no one around to braid it for you, consider the amazing automatic T2 hair machine. Here's how it works: You back your head up to the T2 and turn it on. Your hair is received by the parters that part and pass your hair to the grabbers. The grabbers move your hair in a figure eight while twisting and weaving it into a tight braid. At this point, if all goes according to plan, your hair is released. Wow! Hair today, gone tomorrow.

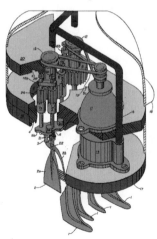

Shocking!

Travel Relief	US Patent No. 5,848,443
	Issue Date 1998

This looks like an invention for the obsessed driver, unwilling to stop for anything. Sometimes when you gotta go, you gotta go, and restrooms be damned, because we're making good time and we're not stopping for anything. We've seen auto urinals before, but this truly is the Cadillac of AUs. Travel Relief isn't just a cup with a lid, oh no. You've got your padded seat receptacle for relief and comfort. You've got your hidden-under-the-seat collecting bladder, and, best of all, this baby flushes! Oh yeah. Push the right button and Ty-D-Bol comes a-flushin'. Push the wrong button, and the storage bladder relieves itself, all over your car.

Shocking!

Smoking more and enjoying it less? Perhaps what you
need is a flavorful Cheese Filtered Cigarette! According
to the inventor, current cigarette filters (circa 1966)
don't filter enough tar and nicotine from tobacco smoke.
He's discovered that cheese makes a very efficient
tobacco filter. But wait! Before you go dipping your
cigarette into last week's leftover, gooey Brie, you need
to follow this simple recipe: Use only a hard cheese such
as Parmesan, Romano, or Swiss. (What, no smoked
Gouda?) Grate the cheese into small pieces and mix with
one-third-part charcoal. The charcoal helps absorb the
cheese oil and keeps the cheese filter from
becoming rancid and odorous
before it reaches your lips.
Hey, now we know
what to do with all of
that government
surplus cheese!

Shocking!

Portable Pet Potty

Many people live in big cities and enjoy the companionship of man's best friend. But with the master working all day, poor Lassie can only count on relief during her morning and evening walks, putting a strain on . . . their relationship. Now it's possible to end canine discomfort with the Portable Pet Potty. This revolutionary invention is made from hermetically sealed polyethylene and is strapped to the heinie of your hound. While this solution may prevent unwanted accidents, don't forget to take Lassie for her walks. The Portable Pet Potty doesn't collect Tootsie Rolls.

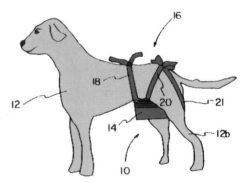

Shocking!